A Rookie reader®

Number One Puppy

Written by Zachary Wilson
Illustrated by Paula Pertile

Children's Press®
A Division of Scholastic Inc.
New York • Toronto • London • Auckland • Sydney
Mexico City • New Delhi • Hong Kong
Danbury, Connecticut

For my niece Elle.
—Z. W.

To Midnite, my own number one puppy.
—P. P.

Reading Consultant

Cecilia Minden-Cupp, PhD
Former Director of the Language and Literacy Program
Harvard Graduate School of Education
Cambridge, Massachusetts

Cover design: The Design Lab
Interior design: Herman Adler

Library of Congress Cataloging-in-Publication Data

Wilson, Zachary, 1975–
  Number one puppy / by Zachary Wilson ; illustrated by Paula Pertile.
    p. cm. — (A rookie reader)
  ISBN 10: 0-531-15475-0 (lib. bdg.)   0-531-12590-4 (pbk.)
  ISBN 13: 978-0-531-15475-5 (lib. bdg.)   978-0-531-12590-8 (pbk.)
  1. Counting—Juvenile literature. I. Title. II. Series.
  QA113.W585 2006
  513.2'11—dc22   2006006795

My mom is taking me to
the pound today. I am going
to bring home a puppy.

There are so many puppies at the pound. How will I pick the one to bring home?

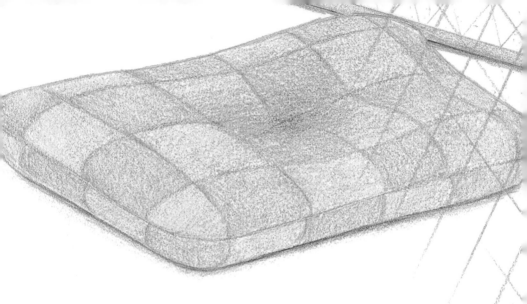

Here is one soft, yellow puppy.
Yellow is my favorite color.
It reminds me of the sun.

Oh! Look at these
two sleepy puppies.
They could snuggle
in my bed.

There are three
black-and-white puppies.
I like their spots.

Here are four quiet
puppies. I bet they can
keep a secret.

There are five fuzzy puppies.
Their fur tickles my nose.

And here are six playful puppies.
I want to run and play with them.

"Please, Mom. I want them all.
How can I pick just one?"
"Only one is the special puppy
just for you," says Mom.

Hmmm. There are six
playful puppies.

There are five fuzzy puppies.

There are four quiet puppies.

There are three
black-and-white puppies.

There are two sleepy puppies.

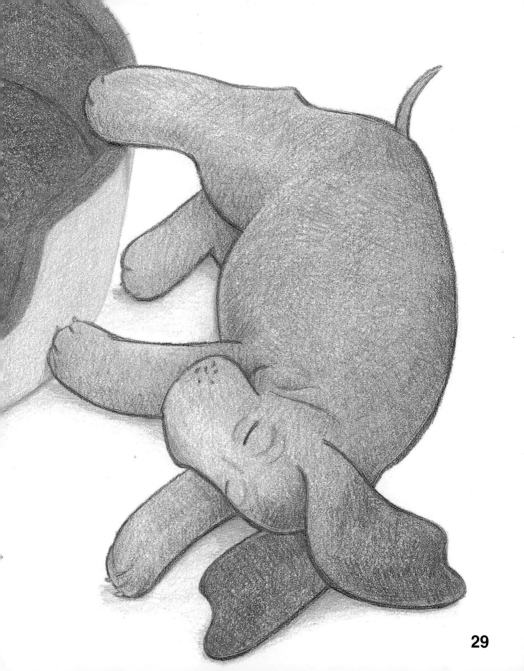

And here is my new
yellow puppy, Sunny.
"Let's go home, Sunny!"

Word List (83 words)

(Words in **bold** are numbers.)

a	fur	many	quiet	their
all	fuzzy	me	reminds	them
am	go	mom	run	there
and	going	my	says	these
are	here	new	secret	they
at	hmmm	nose	**six**	**three**
bed	home	of	sleepy	tickles
bet	how	oh	snuggle	to
black	I	**one**	so	today
bring	in	only	soft	**two**
can	is	pick	special	want
color	it	play	spots	white
could	just	playful	sun	will
favorite	keep	please	Sunny	with
five	let's	pound	taking	yellow
for	like	puppies	the	you
four	look	puppy		

About the Author

Zach Wilson is an art teacher in New Jersey. He enjoys working with children of all ages and looks forward to writing more books.

About the Illustrator

Paula lives in California and still can't believe she gets to draw and color for a living.